Four Essential
Ways that
COACHING
Can Help
EXECUTIVES

Four Essential Ways that Coaching Can Help Executives

Robert Witherspoon
Randall P. White

Center for Creative Leadership
Greensboro, North Carolina

The Center for Creative Leadership is an international, nonprofit educational institution founded in 1970 to advance the understanding, practice, and development of leadership for the benefit of society worldwide. As a part of this mission, it publishes books and reports that aim to contribute to a general process of inquiry and understanding in which ideas related to leadership are raised, exchanged, and evaluated. The ideas presented in its publications are those of the author or authors.

The Center thanks you for supporting its work through the purchase of this volume. If you have comments, suggestions, or questions about any Center publication, please contact John R. Alexander, President, at the address given below.

Center for Creative Leadership
Post Office Box 26300
Greensboro, North Carolina 27438-6300

Center for ®
Creative Leadership
leadership. learning. life.

©1997 Center for Creative Leadership
Reprinted 2001

CCL No. 175

Library of Congress Cataloging-in-Publication Data

Witherspoon, Robert.
    Four essential ways that coaching can help executives / Robert Witherspoon,
    Randall P. White.
            p.   cm.
    Includes bibliographical references (p.   ).
    ISBN 1-882197-26-7
    1. Business consultants. 2. Mentoring in business. 3. Executive ability.
    4. Executives. I. White, Randall P. II. Title.
    HD69.C6W57 1997
    658.4'07124—dc21   97-1375
                                                                                    CIP

For our fathers

Bob Witherspoon, business executive and
enthusiastic entrepreneur

and

George White, military officer and civil servant

We thank you for your constant encouragement and your
leadership by example

Table of Contents

Preface

This paper represents our thinking about executive coaching: what it is, its power in creating behavioral change, and how it can be used by executives and their organizations.

Each of us comes from a different tradition. The first author began in private practice over twenty-five years ago as a consultant and acquired significant business experience along the way, from building small business start-ups to leadership roles in large organizations. (Before founding Performance & Leadership Development, he was a partner in Arthur Andersen.) The second author started in applied social-science research with a focus on executive learning and leadership and has published widely on these and related topics. (He was formerly in charge of executive coaching and customized programs at the Center for Creative Leadership.)

Along the way, each of us gained experience in designing and delivering executive development programs, and each of us held various managerial positions in the course of our careers prior to offering executive coaching as a service. While we work separately, we sometimes compare notes, and over the course of such comparisons have come to spend long hours discussing the roles that coaches can play and the various situations in which these roles unfold.

We discuss here a continuum of roles and situations with several examples. In writing about individuals with whom we have worked, we have tried to remain true to our commitment to keep data private, while at the same time reporting representative coaching situations. To balance these concerns, some changes in the examples were made for this paper by altering characteristics of each case. The actual work was also abbreviated somewhat. The resulting examples therefore should be considered partial composites of representative coaching situations.

Coaching is about bringing out the best in people. Good coaching, we would argue, begins with clarity about roles. Each coaching situation is different, but some distinctions among roles are important to recognize—if only to foster informed choice by everyone: the executive (and possibly family members), the executive's boss, the human resources representative, and the coach (or coaches) providing the service. Our purpose here is to probe key distinguishing factors among the coaching situations we encounter daily in our practice.

Beyond informed choice, we hope this paper fosters a dialogue about the roles coaches play. We see a future where coaching is widely available in organizations, where coaching is informed by insights from an evolving practice theory for coaching executives.

A practice theory resembles formal theory but is based on experience, not systematic research. It constitutes a mental map of what's important and what to do about it. We first learned of "practice theory" from Marvin Weisbord (1987, pp. 260-261), who attributes the concept to Peter Vaill. More recently, Vaill (1989, p. 35) says he meant something very close to the concept of "theory in use" by organizational psychologist Chris Argyris.

We base our practice theory on mental maps drawn up while thinking about a range of coaching cases, such as those presented in this paper. While mental maps paint an incomplete picture of coaching, our aim is to continue clarifying the respective roles of coaching, along with coaching models, best practices, and related matters. We consider this paper to be a work in progress and welcome comments and contributions.

Acknowledgments

The authors wish to acknowledge with thanks the comments and assistance of Richard Beckhard, Teri-E Belf, David DeVries, Arthur Freedman, Mary Kralj, Nick Miles, Donna Morris, Katie White, and Eric Witherspoon.

Introduction

Imagine a professional football team that recruits the best players, puts them through training camp to hone their technical skills and learn the plays and strategies to win, and then plays the entire season without a practice session or a coach. There's not a team owner in the world who would ever expose such a major investment to that kind of risk. Yet most traditional practices in organizations seem to do just that. People are expected to perform key roles—to lead a new project team, to present financial results to outside investors, to manage conflicts across departments—all in an exemplary fashion, without training, practice, or coaching. Consequently, many investments in people—the human side of enterprise—have had mixed results. So many organizations have turned to coaching. Coaching is recognized in business, in teaching, and in sports as a positive and empowering strategy for performance and leadership development.

Effective executive coaching brings out the best in people. The very first use of the word "coach" in English occurred in the 1500s to refer to a particular kind of carriage. (It still does.) Hence, the root meaning of the verb "to coach" is to convey a valued person from where he or she was to where he or she wants to be. That's still a good meaning for coaching executives today (see Evered & Selman, 1989).

For decades, athletes, public speakers, and performing artists have turned to coaches to help them perform better. For individuals already atop their fields, the next level of performance can't be taught, but it can be learned. To coach in these situations is less to instruct than to facilitate (literally, "to make easy"). Now this approach has taken hold in business, where top executives are turning to coaches to reach their business and personal best.

Coaching entails individually helping executives to learn and to make the most of that learning. Because these encounters involve executives in different stages of their careers and in varied settings, coaching represents a continuum of roles. *Sans* role, coaching is a process that helps executives learn, grow, and change. What the coaching involves specifically—whether by Socratic method or multi-rater assessment—depends on the executive and the situation. Coaching is situational, a point captured over a decade ago by Peters and Austin (1985):

In our work with exceptionally talented leaders and coaches, we've discovered that they make dozens of intuitive judgments daily about how to work with their people. Sometimes they focus on removing barriers to performance. Other times they immerse themselves in a situation and exert a great deal of influence on the way it turns out. There are times when they help people work through personal or performance problems, and there are times when the only requirement is to provide straightforward information. In some situations the coach is the dominant figure, while in others the team practically forgets he or she is there. (pp. 398-399)

Experience bears this out with two important exceptions. The first concerns the person coaching. Peters and Austin were talking about leaders and coaches as the same person, typically one's boss or another insider. Since then, a growing number of executives have turned to professional external coaches. According to a recent survey of coaching practices at leading American companies, those coached in business these days "may be anyone from a $60,000 middle manager up to the CEO, although more commonly that person will be a leading contender for the CEO's job" (Smith, 1993). As described in this *Fortune* article, executive coaching involves a skilled outside consultant assigned to an executive on a regular basis for one or more specific functions—to improve the executive's managerial skills; to correct serious performance problems; and/or to facilitate long-term development, often for a future leadership role or top corporate position.

The second exception concerns the exertion of influence. Typically, outside coaches have little or no direct influence—much less control—over the outcome. To have direct control is to manage, not to coach. It is the coach's lack of direct control or authority that makes the coaching task difficult and challenging. A coach, however, can have considerable power depending on reputation, track record, access to other parts of the organization, and so forth. Absence of authority also makes possible major change, because the person being coached must be motivated internally. True, a coach can be instrumental in encouraging or motivating the executive to learn and to change, but ultimately the changes must be embraced by the executive if they are to be effective.

This paper focuses on the specific functions referred to above, called coaching roles. Coaching is more than an event (for example, the feedback day of a leadership development program); it's a continuous process. Good coaching requires a skill, a depth of understanding, and plenty of practice if it is to deliver its remarkable potential. Although some coaches reside inside the organization, this paper addresses the role of external one-on-one coaches in a business context. It does not address other settings, like personal growth seminars or "cyber coaching" over the Internet. Nor does it address group coaching functions like boardroom facilitation and team development. The focus here is on formal coaching—when regular sessions are scheduled and conversations occur—rather than on the many informal opportunities for coaching that arise on a daily basis.[1]

The Roles Consultants Play

Richard Beckhard, considered a founder of organization development, remarks (in conversations December 19, 1994, and March 31, 1995) that he typically plays at least four roles in working with the chief executives, boards, and senior managers of organizations:

- as expert, like a plumber or TV technician, to provide solutions or action recommendations;
- as consultant, to help the client work on a problem, provided that the problem remains the client's responsibility;
- as trainer or educator, to teach the client what he knows, so the client can apply the learning himself; and
- as coach or counselor, to help the client learn and to teach the client how to learn. (For a look at case examples where these roles play out, see Beckhard & Pritchard, 1992.)

The balance of this paper is about this last role—that of executive coach.

The Roles Coaches Play

One way to think of executive coaching roles is in terms of client need. Does the executive need to learn a new skill, to perform better in the present job, or to prepare for a future leadership role? Does the executive understand and acknowledge these needs? Is he or she willing to seek and accept coaching? Or is the executive looking for a confidant to talk through issues and receive constructive feedback before taking action? These questions suggest client need—or primary coaching function—as one key dimension for distinguishing among different coaching roles.

Coaching role refers to the coach's primary function in helping an executive learn, grow, and change. These coaching functions may focus on imparting specific skills, addressing performance issues on the job, or supporting broader changes in the executive's behavior.[2] There are often several coaching functions in any situation, but unless one is defined specifically as primary, there tends to be considerable confusion about expectations and resulting loss of time and effort.

Executive coaching entails several distinctly different roles, based on the primary function:
- coaching for skills (learning sharply focused on a person's current task);
- coaching for performance (learning focused more broadly on a person's present job);
- coaching for development (learning focused on a person's future job); and
- coaching for the executive's agenda (learning focused on the executive's agenda[3] in the broadest sense).

Early in the process, these different executive coaching roles should be clarified and discussed for several reasons.
- It is important for both executive and coach to recognize the distinctions between the various roles, if only to foster informed choice by everyone taking part in the process—the executive (and possibly family members), the executive's boss, the human resources representative, and the coach providing the service.[4]
- These role distinctions provide a common language about coaching for both executives and practitioners and a useful way to orient all parties to the process of assessment, feedback, and action planning.
- These critical distinctions represent a continuing choice through the life of the coaching relationship, but particularly during the early stages. The choices define behaviorally how executives and coaches work together and can make the difference between meeting or not meeting the executive's expectations.[5]
- An open discussion of these matters is helpful in creating some ground rules and a feedback system to be used in the coaching process.

Each of the coaching roles has a different contribution to make when it comes to enabling the executive to act. Role clarity is also key in sizing up the situation: how to approach an opening for coaching; what to emphasize; what to leave alone for the time being; where to start. In practice, of course, these coaching roles may overlap over time. A coach contracted to help in skill building may end up working on performance issues. In the process, a longer-term relationship may be forged that contributes to the executive's overall development. Changes in role, however, should be acknowledged specifically by all parties so the coaching contract can be changed accordingly.

Executive coaching might be defined as a confidential, highly personal learning process. Typically, the coaching is designed to bring about effective action, performance improvement, and/or personal growth for the individual executive, as well as better business results for the executive's organization.[6] More than other forms of organized learning (for example, workshops or traditional classrooms), coaching is personal in several senses. First, it is individualized. In working one-on-one, there is the recognition that no two people are alike. Each person has a unique knowledge base, learning pace, and learning style. Consequently, executives progress at their own pace, although holding people personally accountable for their progress is often a key element of executive coaching. Coaching can be personal in a second sense—by uncovering blind spots and changing one's personal style.

Coaching for Skills

Coaching for skills is learning focused on a person's current task or project, typically in the context of the present job. ("Skill" is used broadly to include basic ideas, strategies, methods, behaviors, attitudes, and perspectives associated with success in business.) Sometimes the executive needs conceptual clarity—"I'm not familiar with the basic principles" or "I don't understand why these skills are needed or when to apply them." Other times the executive needs to build or sharpen a skill associated with success in business or professional life—"I've never learned how to do it" or "I know how, but I don't always do it well."[7] Usually this coaching is needed for the short term (this week, this month) and is clearly identified and agreed on by the executive and others in the organization. Further, coaching for skills represents little or no threat to most learners.

Given that, clarity about the skills to be learned is typically high as perceived by the people considering coaching for skills (the executive, the boss, and others). Coaching goals tend to be clear and specific, at least in the present context. Executives know what's expected of them. The business reasons for coaching are also clear and thoroughly understood by all relevant parties. Consequently, coaching for skills tends to occur over a relatively short period of time.

Compared to other coaching roles, coaching for skills has high clarity, high consensus (people tend to agree about the need for coaching and be strongly committed), and high control (people believe they have a good chance of achieving their learning goals). But of these three characteristics, clarity can be the single most powerful factor to distinguish among coaching roles and can affect the time needed for coaching in many important ways.

Coaching for skills helps people learn specific skills, behaviors, and attitudes—often over several weeks or months. Situations well suited to this coaching role include:

- to support learning on the job (for example, before or after a "first," such as a first customer visit or a first board meeting);
- to support traditional classroom training (for example, by reinforcing learning and practical applications back on the job); or
- to support job redesign (for example, when reengineering introduces new or different roles and responsibilities).

In these cases, the coach helps the executive to size up skill-building needs and to instruct or recommend learning resources that are tailored to these needs. Because the needs are clear and specific, executives can apply their new skills and behaviors promptly. For many executives, time is a key factor. Even if the managing partner in the following example had enjoyed the lead time to attend a course, he might have been reluctant to commit to a three- to five-day executive seminar on advanced presentation skills.

Example

Situation. The managing partner of a worldwide professional services firm was called on—at the last minute—to "pinch hit" for the firm's chairman in a keynote address to roll out the "Vision 2000" program to several thousand partners at the annual meeting. The managing partner understood his presentation skills were a real key but felt uncomfortable talking about a visionary topic to an audience this size and wanted further skills development.

The executive was also unable to turn to someone inside the organization. True, he'd spent years developing management skills, but along the way he'd missed the course on "How to Communicate Your Vision." And the annual meeting was less than sixty days away. Consequently, the managing partner asked an outside coach to help sharpen his presentation skills to enable him to communicate the new vision with clarity and conviction.

Process. The coach began by encouraging the managing partner to talk freely about earlier speaking experiences. Because the coach was an outsider, the executive felt comfortable discussing these matters. In the course of their conversations, it became apparent that most of the managing partner's planning for presentations usually had been the "victim" of last-minute deadlines or competing priorities.

As a result, the coach and the client designed an intensive program organized around weekly coaching sessions over a six-week period. In the first three sessions the executive sharpened his presentation skills and practiced until he had made them his own. These sessions also featured live videotapings of the executive in several speaking situations, along with individualized coaching and critiquing plus written feedback after the coaching sessions. The fourth coaching session included work by the coach and the executive to develop the latter's presentation for the annual meeting. By then, the executive had learned a step-by-step process for planning presentations and left with an outline of his keynote address. Two final sessions allowed time to review the executive's written remarks and to critique the resulting speech rehearsal.

Results. Coaching for skills helped the managing partner better prepare for and deliver this key presentation. He faced the annual meeting with more confidence about the quality of his message and his ability to get the message across. He also felt more in control of both formal and routine speaking situations in the future.

Coaching for Performance

Coaching for performance is learning focused on a person's present job. Typically, the executive feels the need to function more effectively at work ("I need to do a better job at . . .") or to address performance issues ("I'm not aware of how my actions have affected others" or "I have not made a commitment to doing it well"). For executives at risk in the workplace, the challenge may be to correct problem behaviors before they jeopardize productivity or derail a career.[8] Although this coaching is usually seen as needed for the short or intermediate term (this quarter, this year), and it is critical for the long term, it is often seen as less urgently needed than coaching for skills. Also, there may be less shared agreement about the need for performance coaching, particularly with regard to the executive at risk. Finally, coaching for performance can represent more threat to some learners than coaching for skills.[9] For others, the experience is challenging, something like private swimming lessons for Olympic-class swimmers.

In coaching-for-performance situations, clarity is mixed as perceived by those considering the coaching (the executive, the boss, and relevant others). Coaching goals are often fuzzy. For example, there may be a presenting problem ("He's not doing it the way he's supposed to . . .") but little clear definition of actual behavior or root causes. Or people may be expected to improve their effectiveness on their own but don't know how. Likewise, the business reasons for coaching may be less clear than when coaching for skills. Consequently, coaching for performance tends to involve more time, if only to reach clarity and consensus about the need for coaching and desired outcomes.

Coaching for performance helps people improve their effectiveness on the job—often over several quarters or a year or more. This coaching role can be applied to improve performance in a present position:

- to practice and apply effective performance on the job;
- to clarify performance goals when expectations about behavior are unclear or when business goals, roles, or conditions change; or
- to orient and support a newly appointed executive, or someone with significant new responsibilities, in making a smooth transition.

Coaching for performance also can help to change individual behaviors and correct problems:

- to confront ineffective attitudes or other motivational issues;
- to alleviate performance problems when deficiencies jeopardize a person's productivity, job, or career;
- to increase confidence and commitment when seasoned players have experienced career setbacks and disappointments; or
- to deal with blind spots that detract from otherwise outstanding performance.

In these cases, the coach acts as a performance coach by helping executives assess their performance, obtain feedback on individual strengths and weaknesses, and enhance their effectiveness. The coaching sessions typically focus on performance in the present job, although continued improvement may well lead to advancement.

Example

Situation. The CEO of a diversified service firm discovered that as the company grew, there was no performance feedback system to accurately assess his performance or that of other key players in the company. The short-term goal was to set visible measures for executive success and apply them to himself and top managers. Longer term, the CEO hoped to establish a leadership development program that would ensure the next generation of executives for the organization.

Process. A coach was hired to help the CEO achieve these goals. They began by defining a success profile of specific skills and behaviors that related to effectiveness in that organization. Based on this competency model, a multi-rater (360-degree) instrument which best measured these competencies was chosen to gather feedback. An assessment was then conducted in which the executive was reviewed by a full circle of board directors, peers, subordinates, and outside customers whose observations of the CEO could be valuable.

Following the assessment, this feedback was presented, along with the coach's observations of the executive, in a series of confidential sessions. The coach and the executive focused on how to learn from the data by (1) interpreting and accepting the data, (2) identifying performance trends and areas for improvement, (3) analyzing reasons for major performance problems, and (4) establishing action steps for performance improvement.

Results. The CEO described the performance feedback as revealing, accurate, honest, and useful. The feedback was trusted and accepted because it came from the combined judgment of many people with firsthand knowledge of the CEO's performance. With coaching for skills after the assessment, the executive saw progress in managing execution, the skill set he selected to develop. Specifically, he was better able to delegate and coordinate work and was more effective in empowering employees. As a result, both the CEO and others acknowledged that he had become a more effective executive.

Coaching for Development

Coaching for development is learning focused on a person's future job. Typically, the executive needs to prepare for a career move, often as part of succession planning discussions. For some, the challenge may be to strengthen leadership skills for higher levels in the organization. Others may need to "unlearn" a behavior that's become a liability—a strength overdone that has become a weakness. Usually this coaching is needed for the long term (this year, next year). Because coaching for the future is involved, shared agreement about the need for development coaching can be difficult and can vary considerably, from high in organizations with well-honed succession plans and success profiles to low in organizations without them.[10] Finally, coaching for development can be intense, analytical, and may represent more threat to some learners than coaching for skills or performance.[11] Of all the coaching roles, coaching for development tends to involve a deeper focus on executive development *and* personal growth. As one coach has said, "This is easy for people who are introspective and enjoy root canals."

Clarity is low or mixed as perceived by the people considering coaching for development (and because it customarily involves a very senior executive, there can be many relevant others). Clear and specific goals for the coaching may be lacking or at best limited. Predicting future requirements is difficult at best. As a result, it is difficult to specify the future demands to which aspiring executives will have to respond. Consequently, coaching for development tends to involve time, both to reach clarity and consensus and to realize potentially far-reaching changes.

Coaching for development helps people prepare for advancement—often over an extended period of a year or more. Business examples include providing support for possible promotions or lateral transfers. This coaching role can help:

- to learn more skills and capabilities for a future job, after coaching for performance;
- to clarify shared goals about success when executives and their organizations are at odds about the skills and perspectives needed for success in a future position; or
- to encourage the long-term development of promising people by facilitating learning from challenging career experiences.

In these instances, the coach acts as a development coach by helping executives discover their potential to advance and address their long-term development needs—often over several years or an entire career. The coaching sessions typically focus on development for a future job by helping an executive discover strengths and weaknesses, determine where growth is needed and how to fill the gaps.

Example

Situation. A 47-year-old executive vice president of a manufacturing firm had thought about going to a week-long, intensive leadership-development program but could never find the time. With the children in college and his wife beginning to edge back into the workforce, he sensed the time for development was now. In addition, his boss had hinted about changes in the management committee and that he'd be a candidate for one of two positions opening in the next year. According to his boss, better planning and communication skills would improve his current job performance and increase his chances for advancement.

Process. Because of his senior position and his often chaotic schedule, this executive opted for a form of development that would cater to his schedule and specific needs—executive coaching. The data collection took several weeks as interviews were conducted with several superiors, including the immediate boss; about five peers (some of whom were at other subsidiaries); half a dozen subordinates; and spouse, children, siblings, and friends.

All interviews were transcribed and merged into one report where comments were reflected back without attribution but sorted as to source category (i.e., superiors, peers, subordinates). Family data were, however, identified by source, as to do otherwise would be difficult and counterproductive to the development process. These data were then shared with the executive in a concentrated dose over a two-day period of reading, discussing, elaborating on the data, and searching at a cursory level for coherent development themes. (As is often the case for coaching at this level, two coaches were used because of the power of the process and because a pair of coaches could play off each other's insights and interpretive abilities.)

This process provided him with an intense but private look at strengths and developmental needs from multiple sources: interviews using open-ended questions with self, work associates, family, and friends; a 360-degree instrument completed by self and work associates; and several paper-and-pencil inventories for the executive. (Some inventories typically used are the Fundamental Interpersonal Relationship Orientation–Behavior® [FIRO–B®], the Myers-Briggs Type Indicator® [MBTI®], and the California Psychological Inventory® [CPI®]. The process is designed to assist the executive in confirming and clarifying his or her personality preferences and leads to a broader discussion of how these preferences play out in the work setting.) A wealth of data relevant to establishing development priorities was collected.

During follow-up calls and another day-long session a month later, the coaches and the executive prepared a formalized response to the data by answering a series of questions that aid in condensing the data—finding themes and issues to make sense of it all. Typical questions ask the executive to compare patterns of response; for example: Did subordinates see something that peers did not? Did similar themes occur in both family and work data? Is a high need for control, as evidenced in test data, borne out in the workplace or at home?

After another three to four weeks, another meeting was held to formalize a behaviorally specific development plan and to agree on follow-up arrangements. (Who will coach the executive inside the organization during this plan? What will be the spouse's involvement? Which of the two external coaches will follow up and how often? What will it look like when the plan is completed? When will the plan be completed and when will a spot check to assess progress on the plan be done?)

Results. In this case, the changes are still in process. Over the course of the data collection, we discovered that this executive drove himself and everyone around him very hard. Often seen as having his own agenda, being either unable or unwilling to listen, and lacking in appreciative behaviors, the people around the executive were wary of his next promotion. They knew he deserved it but wondered how successful he'd be, given these behaviors.

Interestingly, this behavior played out at home, particularly with a son regarded as very bright and successful in college. The son, while complimentary and supportive of his father, related that his father's high standards for performance had in the last few years gotten in the way of their relationship. In other words, while the executive had conveyed that he valued his son for his academic accomplishment, the son disclosed in the interview, "Dad, you haven't said you love me."

The executive was prepared for the work data he'd received—he'd heard it all before—but not as much the family data. Upon seeing this, the executive was brought up short—"the proverbial 2x4 to the side of the head"—and began to explore in subsequent sessions the impact his behavior had on others, both at home and at work. Through continued work with a coach, and also some important family therapy in his local community, this executive continues to work on those issues identified in this process.

Coaching for the Executive's Agenda

Since an executive's agenda can be broad and evolving, this coaching tends to involve learning in the largest sense. Leading a business or a major business function can be a lonely activity. Often the executive's felt need is for a confidant to offer insight, perspective, and constructive feedback on the executive's ideas. Usually the need for this coaching is ongoing, and coaching sessions evolve in response to the executive's agenda.

Clarity is highly variable as perceived by those considering this coaching (sometimes the executive and only a few others). Sometimes the goal is broad or open-ended. In other cases, the coaching is tied to an organization's priorities—say, to help key people successfully implement specific change initiatives. In any case, the coach—as an objective outsider and "talking partner"—is free to question and engage the executive on major issues, an option less open to corporate insiders. Often a coach in this role also helps the executive obtain valid data to address specific issues or concerns. Consequently, the time involved for this coaching role can be highly variable. Often coaching for the executive's agenda starts with a retainer and evolves into a very long-term relationship. Depending on the executive's agenda, the actual coaching sessions may take place at regular intervals over a specific time period or on an "on call" basis. The threat to learners from this coaching tends to be low, since the executive sets the agenda and controls its content.

Coaching for the executive's agenda helps that person realize broader purposes, the results and well-being the executive wants in life—often on an ongoing basis. The scope for this coaching can range considerably and usually goes beyond a single person or situation. Business examples include: mergers and acquisitions, productivity and quality improvement, executive leadership transitions, turnarounds, and coping with explosive growth. Among the situations well suited to this coaching role are:

- to support better decisions when insight and perspective are needed on an executive's ideas;
- to open up more options when creative suggestions could improve the chances for sound decisions;
- to support change management by preparing an executive to successfully implement specific change initiatives; or
- to guide the executive through unknown or unexplored areas or when the executive feels overwhelmed.

In such instances, the coach acts as a sounding board by offering feedback and suggestions to support or supplement the executive's ideas. Depending on the executive's agenda and scope of coaching, the coach may also act in other capacities, as suggested by the example above. The coach is free to offer suggestions, but the coaching process ensures that executives address the issues and concerns that matter most to them.

Example

Situation. A worldwide financial services firm was rapidly losing market share in one of its business units. Once an industry leader, its competitive position was steadily deteriorating—client service was poor and quality control was marginal. To compound problems, the company's highly centralized and bureaucratic decision-making was ineffective in responding to its new environment.

The executive in charge realized the business unit had to change, starting with a strategic commitment to provide its clients with the very best service available. Beyond developing a specific change strategy, the challenge was to win the commitment of the people and involve them in all levels of the change effort. The executive needed to move quickly and decisively to diffuse employee fears about firm-wide downsizing.

Process. The executive engaged a coach to help her lead this change. She wanted an experienced sounding board, because her own exposure to changing organizations had convinced her that it was much more difficult to implement strategy than to develop it. And she wanted an objective outside resource as she worked through the toughest issues. The coach began by helping the executive clarify her own goals for change, as well as the roles she wished to play in the change process.

In conjunction with the organization's human resources department, the coach helped the executive assess the situation in a systematic way. Attitude surveys and structured interviews were employed to diagnose key issues and set an agenda for change. A "balanced scorecard" was developed to measure progress on a regular basis, covering client service, cost effectiveness, improved teamwork, and related performance ratings.

To support the executive and the organization, the coach also facilitated a strategic retreat—a first for this business unit. The two-day meeting resulted in a new direction, a reallocation of resources to foster client service and teamwork, and a broad commitment to a longer-term change effort. In partnership, the coach and the executive designed several pilot projects to continue the change.

At the executive's request, the members of one team received further coaching to strengthen client service by redefining their traditional work roles and responsibilities, delegating more authority to the field, and restructuring their $120 million loan portfolio. The new team was supported with facilitation and more managers, and staff specialists were trained to sharpen their group skills and foster teamwork. Management meetings and reinforcement sessions were conducted to increase the impact of this training.

Throughout the change, the executive was coached and was provided with feedback about her performance in leading the effort, based on direct observation of her behavior in work settings and interviews of co-workers about her effectiveness as a leader and manager. Like many forms of performance feedback, comments from co-workers were provided on an anonymous—or not for attribution—basis. Meanwhile, the coach remained on call to assist the executive's change effort.

Results. In just a year, remarkable changes had occurred in the business unit. "We have improved our performance substantially," said the executive, "and with lower operating costs." Senior management agreed, and the organization's board approved a major new commitment to the business unit in record time.

Meanwhile, the emphasis on client service is expanding throughout the unit. Teams have gained more authority and ownership, and the operation has gone from an autocratic managerial style to a participative one. At its next strategic retreat, the executive and her managers and staff noted numerous changes for the better—including their ability to adapt—and renewed their commitment to continuing the change effort into the new year. Headquarters has taken notice of the improved teamwork and put forth the business unit as a model for the larger organization.

The executive continues to talk about what she learned from the coaching, about the key differences between her leading change and managing execution, and how she can now perform both roles better.

Conclusion: Some Similarities in Coaching

In this paper we focused on some significant distinctions among coaching roles. But we want to close by pointing out that all coaching roles have some things in common. First, all executive coaching involves action research—or action learning, the "user friendly" term.[12] Second, successful coaching involves working in partnership with executives. By combining a coach's observations and capabilities (especially the ability to ask effective questions) with an executive's expertise, the executive achieves better and faster results. Typically, the coaching process involves the following steps:

- *Commitment:* to contract for coaching. The coach, the executive, and the executive's boss or human resources professional meet to set the coaching agenda and arrange next steps.
- *Assessment:* to set a goal or define a problem, however fuzzy. In this step, coach and executive also help determine the difference between the executive's goals and reality—the distance between where the executive is and where the executive wants to be. The size of and reason for the gap are discussed. Assessment can be as simple as a series of conversations or as complex as an extensive data-collection effort. No two situations are alike. The result of this step is a clear and realistic plan of action.
- *Action:* to help implement change in the way the executive thinks and performs by building competence, confidence, and commitment. This is where the other coaching roles come into play. If coaching for the executive's agenda, the actions could include interventions at the group and organization level (for example, team building and strategic planning). In some cases, these services are offered by the coach; in others, additional resources are recommended.
- *Continuous improvement:* to assure that the actions are achieving the desired results. To ensure ongoing impact, methods to monitor and sustain successes over time can also be created.

As such, executive coaching is a data-based action-research approach inasmuch as it combines feedback data and research on individual executives with consulting services to the executive.

Notes

1. "Formal coaching" starts with clear contracting about specific expectations (for example, coaching goals and roles), entered into with mutual consent and for valid consideration. Sometimes, however, even formal coaching occurs on the fly, as when a coach shadows the executive to directly observe the client in work settings (for example, plant inspections or staff meetings). Typically, the goals for this coaching are to observe the client in action and/or to hear what others say about him. In our experience, such coaching interventions can be very valuable. Often, this additional knowledge from direct observation, when brought back into the coaching sessions, enriches the executive's options and opens up certain problem areas to more concrete discussion. For an exploration and case examples of such coaching, see Schein (1969), especially pages 167-172. As he points out, the selection of a setting (i.e., what and when to observe) in which to work is an early choice that needs to be addressed collaboratively with the client.

2. Some coaches would also argue that coaching allows executives to undergo a character shift and profound personal changes—such as by moderating a drive for perfectionism or the need to overcontrol (see Kaplan, Drath, & Kofodimos, 1991).

3. We use the term "executive's agenda" in a sense similar to John Kotter's (1982) "agenda setting." He used this term deliberately to distinguish between the ways general managers actually determine direction and the formal strategic-planning process in many organizations. The former, he found, contained "loosely connected goals and plans" addressing a range of time frames covering a broad range of business issues and included both "vague and specific goals and plans" (p. 66). In its broadest sense, this coaching might be considered "coaching for purpose." For ideas about incorporating life purpose into coaching practice, see Belf (1996).

4. In our practice, we use "executive" and "client" interchangeably as the primary person receiving coaching. Often this person is distinct from the "customer" or "client system," terms for the organization that contracts for coaching and pays for the service. Particularly when these parties are different, it is important to clarify at the outset whose interests the coach is serving—the client or the customer—and to follow other safeguards for all parties. We favor disclosing and discussing these issues in advance and

managing the process by establishing a clear contract with the executive and the company as to the coach's role, the purpose of any assessments, the nature and extent of reporting relationships, and so forth.

5. For example, when coaching for skills, a coach might plan in detail what is wanted of learners, convey instructions carefully, repeat key points, encourage note taking, etc. When coaching for performance, a coach might encourage the learner to play a larger role in all these activities, offering support and assistance when necessary—often in the form of a question or suggestion rather than a specific proposal. Effective coaches also recognize that learners vary in their capacity to cope with ambiguity. They therefore attempt to give learners the right mix of direction and choice, so as to avoid either over-direction or open-endedness.

6. A related definition, adopted by the Professional and Personal Coaches Association, sees coaching as "an ongoing relationship which focuses on the client taking action toward the realization of their vision, goals or desires. Coaching uses a process of inquiry and personal discovery to build the client's level of awareness and responsibility and provides the client with structure, support and feedback." See "Being in Action" (1995).

7. This includes competencies required at increasing levels of responsibility. For example, basic management skills might be planning, organizing, setting priorities and so forth, while advanced skills associated with success in middle management could include conflict management, customer focus, and delegating skills. Skills associated with success in the executive suite might include political savvy, strategic agility, and managing vision and purpose. Many basic and advanced skills would need to be fairly solid in order to develop executive skills at this level.

8. We call this related coaching subrole "coaching to correct performance" or "coaching for turnaround" ("fix-its" for short). It involves interventions designed to remedy problems that interfere with the person's job performance. These problems are often considered to be motivational or attitudinal. Like coaching for performance, the primary focus is the present job, but the process of coaching to correct performance may be different for several reasons. For one thing, much more time may be spent clarifying the problem with the executive and the boss. Unless both agree that a problem

exists and that its cause is clear, and unless both are committed to address the issue, little is likely to be accomplished.

9. An obvious reason concerns the executive at risk, who may see the coaching as remedial or as a reflection on the executive's standing in the company. Less obvious, perhaps, is the case of a strong performer who may be ambivalent about being coached. These mixed feelings can take the form of overdependence—getting the coach to make the decisions, so that if something goes wrong the client knows who to blame.

10. As a practical matter, an early step in coaching for development is often to help executives and their organizations clarify the skills and competencies for success in a future executive job or leadership role. The resulting success profile (also known as a competency model) defines sets of skills and behaviors shown by research and experience to be strongly related to effective performance in management, leadership, and executive positions.

11. Coaching for development can represent a relatively greater threat to the learner than other coaching roles for several reasons. For starters, the data collection and feedback for this form of coaching goes well beyond standard 360-degree assessments on two counts—the amount and type of data collected. (This "enhanced feedback" can include data from the workplace, data from personal life, data on behavior and motivation, and information on the present as well as past history of the executive.) Also, there is a strong emphasis on implementation. Consequently, the resulting feedback is powerful—and potentially harmful (what one person called an "emotional boot camp"). While permanent harm rarely is caused by such feedback, certain steps should be followed and certain precautions taken to minimize the risks. For a discussion of these issues, along with many sensible suggestions, see Kaplan and Palus (1994).

12. *Action research* is research on action with the goal of making that action more effective. Conceived as a novel form of problem solving by social psychologist Kurt Lewin, this "learning by doing" approach is now widely practiced in organizational change and development efforts. *Action learning,* a more recent term, is precisely what it sounds like—learning by experience, through solving real business problems in unfamiliar situations when there is a real need for a solution. Originally conceived by a British professor, Reginald Revans, action learning first gained popularity in England

and Europe as an effective way to develop executives and then arrived in North America as a means of business problem solving and management development to the benefit of both the corporation and the participant. (For detailed descriptions of action research, see Shepard's model [in French & Bell, 1990], and Weisbord, 1987. For an early account of action learning, see Foy, 1977.)

References

Beckhard, R., & Pritchard, W. (1992). *Changing the essence: The art of creating and leading fundamental change in organizations.* San Francisco: Jossey-Bass.

Being in action. (1995, Autumn). *The Journal of Professional and Personal Coaching,* p. 1.

Belf, T. (1996, Spring). In the beginning . . . on purpose. In "Being in Action," *The Journal of Professional and Personal Coaching*, p. 4.

Evered, R. D., & Selman, J. C. (1989). Coaching and the art of management. *Organizational Dynamics, 18*(2), 16-32.

Foy, N. (1977, September-October). Action learning comes to industry. *Harvard Business Review*, pp. 158-168.

French, W. L., & Bell, C. H., Jr. (Eds.). (1990). *Organization development: Behavioral science interventions for organization improvement* (p. 102). Englewood Cliffs, NJ: Prentice Hall.

Kaplan, R. E., Drath, W. H., & Kofodimos, J. R. (1991). *Beyond ambition: How driven managers can lead better and live better.* San Francisco: Jossey-Bass.

Kaplan, R. E., & Palus, C. J. (1994). *Enhancing 360-degree feedback for senior executives: How to maximize the benefits and minimize the risks.* Greensboro, NC: Center for Creative Leadership.

Kotter, J. P. (1982). *The general managers.* New York: Free Press.

Peters, T. J., & Austin, N. K. (1985). *A passion for excellence: The leadership difference.* New York: Warner Books.

Schein, E. H. (1969). *Process consultation: Its role in organization development.* Reading, MA: Addison-Wesley.

Smith, L. (1993, December 27). The executive's new coach. *Fortune*, pp. 126-134.

Vaill, P. (1989). *Managing as a performing art.* San Francisco: Jossey-Bass.

Weisbord, M. R. (1987). *Productive workplaces: Organizing and managing for dignity, meaning, and community.* San Francisco: Jossey-Bass.

Suggested Readings

Consulting Psychology Journal: Practice & Research, 1996, *48*(2), 57-152.

The ten articles comprising this special issue are devoted to exploring executive coaching—what it is, how it's done, why it's important, and how it might be improved. According to guest editor Richard R. Kilburg, the issue was designed "to provide an opportunity for leading practitioners to describe what they are doing and help define the core concepts and definitions of this emerging competency." Cases give concrete examples for executives, coaches, and human resources professionals.

[This is probably the best single source about coaching theory and practice today.]

Fournies, F. (1978). *Coaching for improved work performance*. New York: Van Nostrand Reinhold.

This book focuses on coaching as a management function, starting with a sound diagnosis of performance issues. It includes a step-by-step coaching model that emphasizes asking questions to involve the person coached in both discovering performance gaps and in developing concrete solutions. Sample coaching dialogues demonstrate how a coach can focus discussions on future actions (versus such potentially unproductive topics as assigning blame or creating explanations or excuses for past behavior).

[This book can be helpful for both managers and executives who coach and for human resources professionals.]

Hughes, R., Ginnett, R. C., & Curphy, G. J. (1996). *Leadership: Enhancing the lessons of experience* (2nd ed.). Chicago: Irwin, pp. 216-238.

This is a leadership textbook authored by three psychologists, and thus reflects the distinctive perspective of their discipline. It presents a model for changing managerial behavior that features coaching to facilitate individual change. It also reviews research about changing the behavior of executives, notably through coaching sessions designed for a wide range of participants—from successful executives who need one or two key leadership skills, to high potentials with a few "rough edges," to others at risk of derailing in their careers. It concludes that a solid body of research shows that well-designed and executed coaching can result in permanent behavior changes for the better.

[This is the latest edition of a popular text with a wealth of insight and information. It includes clear text and thought-provoking sidebars, along with well-considered discussion questions and suggested readings.]

Kaplan, R. E., & Palus, C. P. (1994). *Enhancing 360-degree feedback for senior executives: How to maximize the benefits and minimize the risks.* Greensboro, NC: Center for Creative Leadership.

This publication explores the risks and benefits of "enhanced 360-degree feedback" for senior executives, including a richer feedback experience, an extended coaching relationship, and other features that go well beyond prior coaching practices. It includes guidelines and suggestions for how enhanced feedback can be provided safely and effectively.

[This can be particularly helpful for human resources professionals and executives considering this form of coaching for development.]

LaMountain, D. (1986). *Executive coaching: Cost-effective, one-on-one guided development strategies* [Audiotape]. Alexandria, VA: American Society for Training & Development.

This is an audiotape, with audience participation, about introducing executive coaching into organizations. The ensuing discussion reviews a wide range of executive coaching issues, primarily from the perspective of corporate human-resources officers. Topics include: typical training department roles in developing executive talent; limitations of group training for executives; possible barriers in introducing one-on-one coaching in organizations; typical coaching issues when getting started; profile of a "good" coaching candidate; and factors to consider when choosing internal and external coaching staff.

[This tape can be helpful for human resources professionals considering the use of coaching for their executives, using either internal or external resources.]

Lary, B. (1997, January). Executive counsel. *Human Resource Executive*, pp. 46-49.

This article explores the growing use of qualified outside coaches for executives, based on interviews with corporate human-resources executives and coaching practitioners. It reviews key business reasons for executive coaching, typical steps and time frames, and costs; it concludes with tips and cautions for selecting a coach.

[This is a good article for human resources professionals looking for coaching resources outside their organizations.]

Mace, M. L. (1950). *The growth and development of executives.* Boston: Division of Research, Graduate School of Business Administration, Harvard University.

This is one of the first works about coaching as a management function, part of the boss's responsibility to develop subordinates through daily efforts to modify and reinforce desired behaviors. Interested readers may also want to consult "On-the-job Coaching" by M. L. Mace and W. R. Mahler in *Developing Executive Skills* (edited by H. F. Merrill & E. Marting, New York: American Management Association, 1958).

Schein, E. H. (1988). *Process consultation: Its role in organization development* (Rev. ed.). Reading, MA: Addison-Wesley, pp. 167-176.

The revised edition of this 1969 classic explores coaching as a professional function, usually carried out by human resources officers or a skilled outside coach assigned to the executive. The cases contain many useful cautions and suggestions for effective coaching.

Tristram, C. (1996, October-November). Wanna be a player? Get a coach! *Fast Company,* pp. 145-150.

The focus in this article is on finding a personal coach, including examples (championship coaches for peak performance, drill coaches for up-and-comers, and the relief coach for entry-level employees) and suggestions about how to get the most from your coach.

[This should be helpful for people considering personal coaching, as well as for aspiring personal coaches.]

Waldroof, J., & Butler, T. (1996, November-December). The executive as coach. *Harvard Business Review*, pp. 111-117.

Written mainly for executives, this article explores some of the typical openings for coaching in the workplace, as well as the reluctance of some executives to coach. It suggests effective questions to ask when evaluating a situation, assessing problem behaviors, and calibrating the executive's own coaching abilities.

[This article is especially helpful for executives trying to do a better job at coaching their people.]

Whitmore, J. (1996). *Coaching for performance: A practical guide to growing your own skills.* London: Nicholas Brealey Publishing.

This publication is a practical introduction to coaching, from the sports origins of coaching to current business applications. It is authored by a co-founder of Inner Game Ltd., which has been highly influential in introducing new coaching approaches in Europe. It provides a coaching method that uses questions rather than instructions. It follows the GROW sequence—goals, reality, options, will—to generate prompt action and peak performance. It also contains a table of standard questions that could form the basis of a coaching session or be tailored to a particular situation.

[This easy-to-use handbook is an excellent way to learn coaching on one's own, starting with self-coaching.]

CENTER FOR CREATIVE LEADERSHIP PUBLICATIONS LIST

NEW RELEASES

IDEAS INTO ACTION GUIDEBOOKS

Ongoing Feedback: How to Get It, How to Use It Kirkland & Manoogian (1998, Stock #400) $8.95*

Reaching Your Development Goals McCauley & Martineau (1998, Stock #401) $8.95

Becoming a More Versatile Learner Dalton (1998, Stock #402) $8.95

Giving Feedback to Subordinates Buron & McDonald-Mann (1999, Stock #403) $8.95*

Three Keys to Development: Using Assessment, Challenge, and Support to Drive Your Leadership Browning & Van Velsor (1999, Stock #404) $8.95

Feedback That Works: How to Build and Deliver Your Message Weitzel (2000, Stock #405) $8.95*

Communicating Across Cultures Prince & Hoppe (2000, Stock #406) $8.95

Learning From Life: Turning Life's Lessons into Leadership Experience Ruderman & Ohlott (2000, Stock #407) $8.95

Keeping Your Career on Track: Twenty Success Strategies Chappelow & Leslie (2001, Stock #408) $8.95

Preparing for Development: Making the Most of Formal Leadership Programs Martineau & Johnson (2001, Stock #409) $8.95

Choosing Executives: A Research Report on the Peak Selection Simulation Deal, Sessa, & Taylor (1999, Stock #183) $20.00*

Coaching for Action: A Report on Long-term Advising in a Program Context Guthrie (1999, Stock #181) $20.00*

The Complete Inklings: Columns on Leadership and Creativity Campbell (1999, Stock #343) $30.00

Discovering the Leader in You Lee & King (2001, Stock #2067) $32.95

Executive Coaching: An Annotated Bibliography Douglas & Morley (2000, Stock #347) $20.00

Executive Selection: Strategies for Success Sessa & Taylor (2000, Stock #2057) $34.95*

Geographically Dispersed Teams: An Annotated Bibliography Sessa, Hansen, Prestridge, & Kossler (1999, Stock #346) $20.00

High-Performance Work Organizations: Definitions, Practices, and an Annotated Bibliography Kirkman, Lowe, & Young (1999, Stock #342) $20.00

The Human Side of Knowledge Management: An Annotated Bibliography Mayer (2000, Stock #349) $20.00

Internalizing Strengths: An Overlooked Way of Overcoming Weaknesses in Managers Kaplan (1999, Stock #182) $15.00

Leadership and Spirit Moxley (1999, Stock #2035) $32.95

Leadership Resources: A Guide to Training and Development Tools (8th ed.) Schwartz & Gimbel (2000, Stock #348) $49.95*

Positive Turbulence: Developing Climates for Creativity, Innovation, and Renewal Gryskiewicz (1999, Stock #2031) $32.95

Selecting International Executives: A Suggested Framework and Annotated Bibliography London & Sessa (1999, Stock #345) $20.00

Workforce Reductions: An Annotated Bibliography Hickok (1999, Stock #344) $20.00

BEST-SELLERS

Breaking Free: A Prescription for Personal and Organizational Change Noer (1997, Stock #271) $25.00

Breaking the Glass Ceiling: Can Women Reach the Top of America's Largest Corporations? (Updated Edition) Morrison, White, & Van Velsor (1992, Stock #236A) $13.00

The Center for Creative Leadership Handbook of Leadership Development McCauley, Moxley, & Van Velsor (Eds.) (1998, Stock #201) $70.00*

CEO Selection: A Street-smart Review Hollenbeck (1994, Stock #164) $12.50*

Choosing 360: A Guide to Evaluating Multi-rater Feedback Instruments for Management Development Van Velsor, Leslie, & Fleenor (1997, Stock #334) $15.00*

Eighty-eight Assignments for Development in Place Lombardo & Eichinger (1989, Stock #136) $15.00*

Enhancing 360-degree Feedback for Senior Executives: How to Maximize the Benefits and Minimize the Risks Kaplan & Palus (1994, Stock #160) $7.50*

Evolving Leaders: A Model for Promoting Leadership Development in Programs Palus & Drath (1995, Stock #165) $15.00

Executive Selection: A Research Report on What Works and What Doesn't Sessa, Kaiser, Taylor, & Campbell (1998, Stock #179) .... $30.00 *

Feedback to Managers (3rd Edition) Leslie & Fleenor (1998, Stock #178) .... $30.00 *

Four Essential Ways that Coaching Can Help Executives Witherspoon & White (1997, Stock #175) $10.00

High Flyers: Developing the Next Generation of Leaders McCall (1997, Stock #293) $27.95

How to Design an Effective System for Developing Managers and Executives Dalton & Hollenbeck (1996, Stock #158) .... $15.00 *

If I'm In Charge Here, Why Is Everybody Laughing? Campbell (1984, Stock #205) .... $9.95 *

If You Don't Know Where You're Going You'll Probably End Up Somewhere Else Campbell (1974, Stock #203) .... $9.95 *

International Success: Selecting, Developing, and Supporting Expatriate Managers Wilson & Dalton (1998, Stock #180) .... $15.00 *

The Lessons of Experience: How Successful Executives Develop on the Job McCall, Lombardo, & Morrison (1988, Stock #211) $27.50

Making Common Sense: Leadership as Meaning-making in a Community of Practice Drath & Palus (1994, Stock #156) $15.00

Managing Across Cultures: A Learning Framework Wilson, Hoppe, & Sayles (1996, Stock #173) $15.00

Maximizing the Value of 360-degree Feedback Tornow, London, & CCL Associates (1998, Stock #295) .... $44.95 *

Perspectives on Dialogue: Making Talk Developmental for Individuals and Organizations Dixon (1996, Stock #168) $20.00

Preventing Derailment: What To Do Before It's Too Late Lombardo & Eichinger (1989, Stock #138) $25.00

The Realities of Management Promotion Ruderman & Ohlott (1994, Stock #157) .... $7.50 *

Selected Research on Work Team Diversity Ruderman, Hughes-James, & Jackson (Eds.) (1996, Stock #326) $24.95

Should 360-degree Feedback Be Used Only for Developmental Purposes? Bracken, Dalton, Jako, McCauley, Pollman, with Preface by Hollenbeck (1997, Stock #335) .... $15.00 *

Take the Road to Creativity and Get Off Your Dead End Campbell (1977, Stock #204) .... $9.95 *

Twenty-two Ways to Develop Leadership in Staff Managers Eichinger & Lombardo (1990, Stock #144) $15.00

BIBLIOGRAPHIES

Formal Mentoring Programs in Organizations: An Annotated Bibliography Douglas (1997, Stock #332) $20.00

Management Development through Job Experiences: An Annotated Bibliography McCauley & Brutus (1998, Stock #337) $10.00

Selection at the Top: An Annotated Bibliography Sessa & Campbell (1997, Stock #333) .... $20.00 *

Succession Planning: An Annotated Bibliography Eastman (1995, Stock #324) .... $20.00 *

Using 360-degree Feedback in Organizations: An Annotated Bibliography Fleenor & Prince (1997, Stock #338) .... $15.00 *

SPECIAL PACKAGES

Executive Selection Package (Stock #710C; includes 157, 164, 179, 180, 183, 333, 345, 2057) $100.00

Feedback Guidebook Package (Stock #724; includes 400, 403, 405) $17.95

Human Resources Professionals Information Package (Stock #717C; includes 136, 158, 179, 180, 181, 201, 324, 334, 348—includes complimentary copy of guidebook 407) $150.00

Personal Growth, Taking Charge, and Enhancing Creativity (Stock #231; includes 203, 204, 205) ... $25.00

The 360 Collection (Stock #720C; includes 160, 178, 295, 334, 335, 338—includes complimentary copy of guidebook 400) $100.00

*Indicates publication is also part of a package.

ORDER FORM

Or e-mail your order via the Center's online bookstore at www.ccl.org

Name _____ Title _____

Organization _____

Mailing Address _____
(street address required for mailing)

City/State/Zip _____

Telephone _____ FAX _____
(telephone number required for UPS mailing)

Quantity	Stock No.	Title	Unit Cost	Amount

CCL's Federal ID Number is 237-07-9591.

Subtotal	
Shipping and Handling (add 6% of subtotal with a $4.00 minimum; add 40% on all international shipping)	
NC residents add 6% sales tax; CA residents add 7.5% sales tax; CO residents add 6% sales tax	
TOTAL	

METHOD OF PAYMENT
(ALL orders for less than $100 must be PREPAID.)

❏ Check or money order enclosed (payable to Center for Creative Leadership).

❏ Purchase Order No. _____ (Must be accompanied by this form.)

❏ Charge my order, plus shipping, to my credit card:
       ❏ American Express   ❏ Discover   ❏ MasterCard   ❏ Visa

ACCOUNT NUMBER: _____ EXPIRATION DATE: MO.___ YR.___

NAME OF ISSUING BANK: _____

SIGNATURE _____

❏ Please put me on your mailing list.

Publication • Center for Creative Leadership • P.O. Box 26300
Greensboro, NC 27438-6300
336-545-2810 • FAX 336-282-3284

Client Priority Code: R

fold here

_____

_____

_____

CENTER FOR CREATIVE LEADERSHIP
PUBLICATION
P.O. Box 26300
Greensboro, NC 27438-6300